HAL•LEONARD

Pro Vocal

BETTER THAN KARAOKE!

SONGBOOK & SOUND-ALIKE CD
WITH UNIQUE *PITCH-CHANGER*™

WOMEN / MEN EDITION

VOLUME 7

Christmas Carols

ISBN 978-1-4234-8322-9

HAL•LEONARD®
CORPORATION
7777 W. BLUEMOUND RD. P.O. BOX 13819 MILWAUKEE, WI 53213

In Australia Contact:
Hal Leonard Australia Pty. Ltd.
4 Lentara Court
Cheltenham, Victoria, 3192 Australia
Email: ausadmin@halleonard.com

Visit Hal Leonard Online at
www.halleonard.com

Hark! The Herald Angels Sing

Words by Charles Wesley
Altered by George Whitefield
Music by Felix Mendelssohn-Bartholdy
Arranged by William H. Cummings

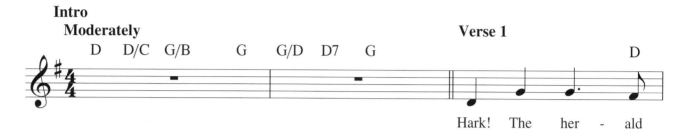

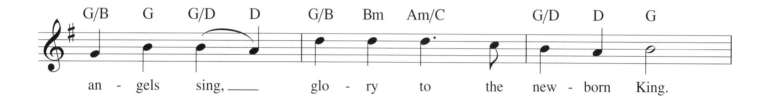

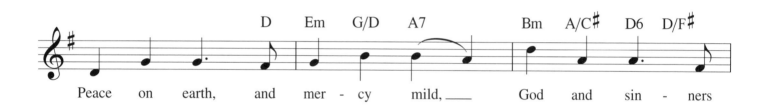

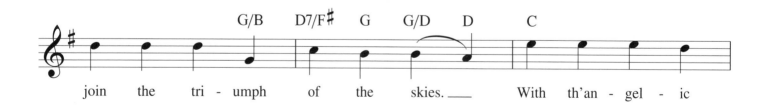

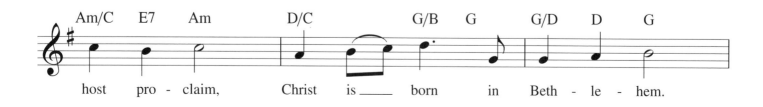

Verse 3

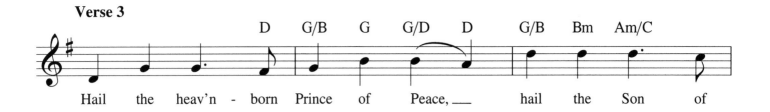

Hail the heav'n-born Prince of Peace, ___ hail the Son of

Right - eous - ness. Light and life to all he brings, ___

ris'n with heal - ing in his wings. Mild he lays his

glo - ry by, ___ born that man no more may die. ___

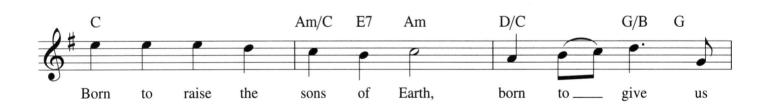

Born to raise the sons of Earth, born to ___ give us

sec - ond birth. Hark, the her - ald an - gels sing,

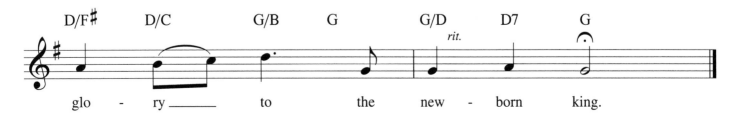

glo - ry ___ to the new - born king.

6

It Came Upon The Midnight Clear

Words by Edmund Hamilton Sears
Music by Richard Storrs Willis

Intro
Moderately

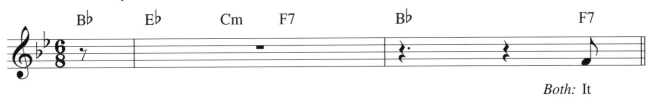

Both: It

Verse 1

came up - on ___ the mid - night clear, that glo - rious song ___ of

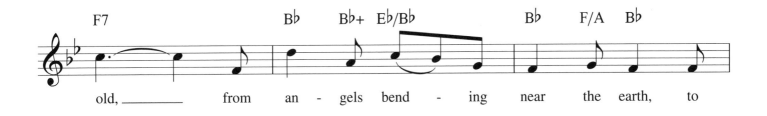

old, ___ from an - gels bend - ing near the earth, to

touch their harps ___ of gold. ___ Peace on the earth, ___ good-

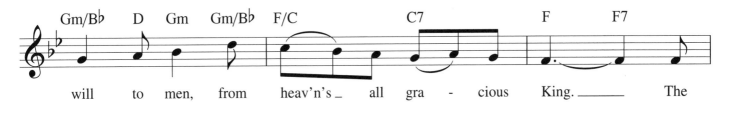

will to men, from heav'n's ___ all gra - cious King. ___ The

world in sol - emn still - ness lay, to hear the an - gels

Verse 2

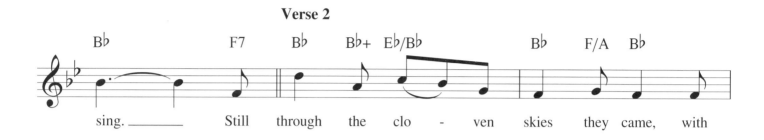

sing. _____ Still through the clo - ven skies they came, with

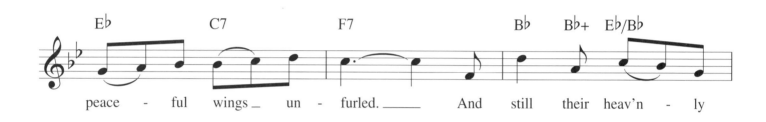

peace - ful wings __ un - furled. _____ And still their heav'n - ly

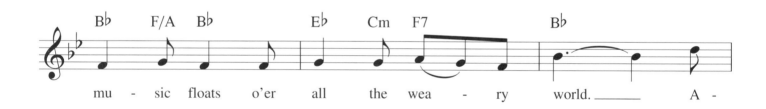

mu - sic floats o'er all the wea - ry world. _____ A -

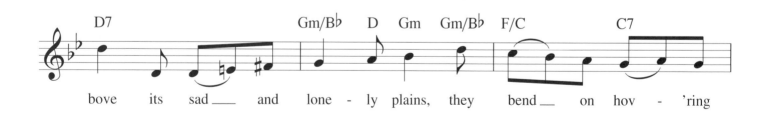

bove its sad __ and lone - ly plains, they bend __ on hov - 'ring

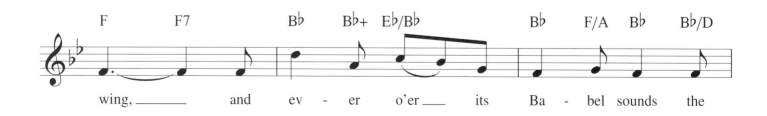

wing, _____ and ev - er o'er __ its Ba - bel sounds the

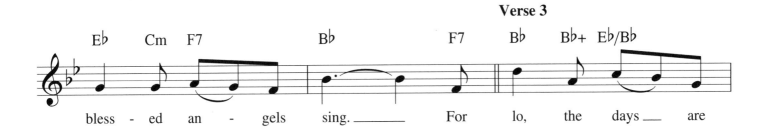

bless - ed an - gels sing. _____ For lo, the days ___ are

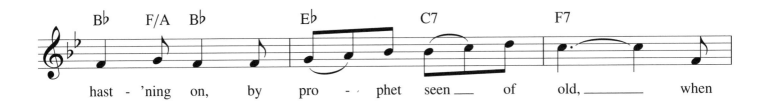

hast - 'ning on, by pro - phet seen ___ of old, _____ when

with the ev - er - cir - cling years comes now the age ___ of

gold. _____ When peace shall o - ver all the earth its

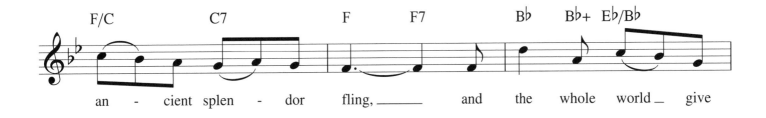

an - cient splen - dor fling, _____ and the whole world ___ give

back the song which now the ang - els sing. _____

Joy To The World

Words by Isaac Watts
Music by George Frideric Handel
Adapted by Lowell Mason

Intro
Majestically

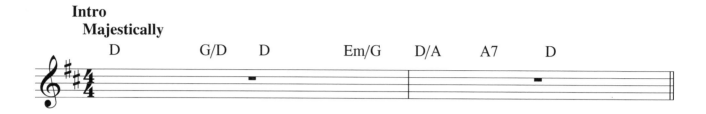

Verse 1

Joy to the world, the Lord is come. Let Earth re- ceive her

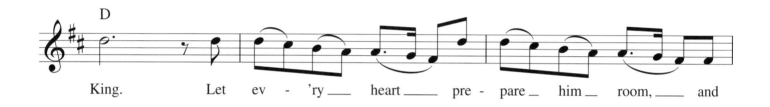

King.   Let ev - 'ry ___ heart ___ pre - pare ___ him ___ room, ___ and

heav'n and na - ture ___ sing,   and ___ heav'n and na - ture ___ sing,   and ___

Verse 2

heav'n, _ and heav'n ___ and na - ture sing.   Joy to the world, the

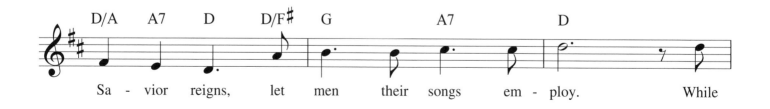

Sa - vior reigns,   let men their songs em - ploy.   While

fields — and — floods, — rocks, hills — and — plains — re -

A7

peat the sound - ing — joy, re - peat the sound - ing — joy, re -

Verse 3

D G/D D Em/G D/A A7 D Em/G

peat, — re - peat — the sound - ing joy. He rules the world with

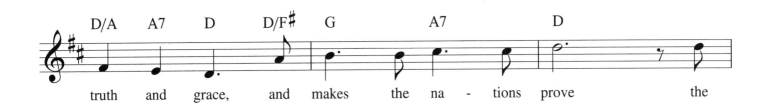

D/A A7 D D/F# G A7 D

truth and grace, and makes the na - tions prove the

glo - ries — of — his right - eous - ness, — and

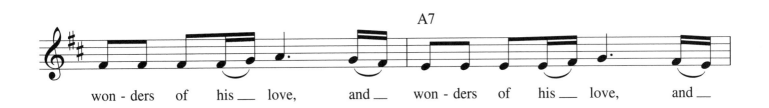

A7

won - ders of his — love, and — won - ders of his — love, and —

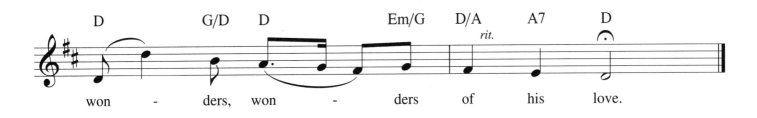

D G/D D Em/G D/A A7 D
rit.

won - ders, won - ders of his love.

O Come, All Ye Faithful
(Adeste Fideles)

Music by John Francis Wade
Latin Words translated by Frederick Oakeley

Intro
Moderately

Verse 1

O come, all ye faith - ful,

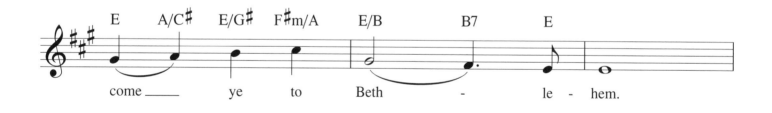

joy - ful and tri - um - phant. O come, ye, o

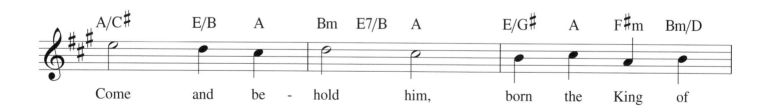

come ____ ye to Beth - le - hem.

Come and be - hold him, born the King of

an - gels. O come, let us a - dore him. O

Verse 3

Christ _____ the Lord. A - des - te Fi -

de - les, lae - ti tri - um - phan - tes. Ve -

ni - te, ve - ni - te in Beth - le -

hem. Na - tum vi - de - te, Re - gem An - ge -

lor - um. Ve - ni - te a - do - re - mus, ve -

ni - te a - do - re - mus, ve - ni - te a - do -

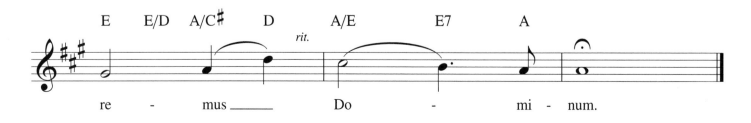

re - mus _____ Do - mi - num.

O Come, O Come Immanuel

Plainsong, 13th Century
Words translated by John M. Neale and Henry S. Coffin

Intro
Slowly and peacefully

Verse 1

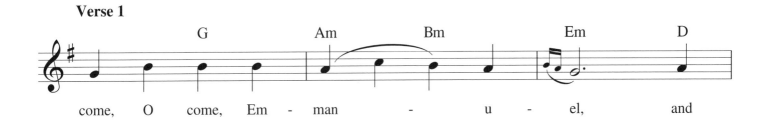

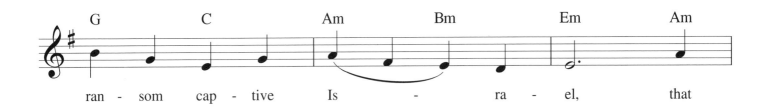

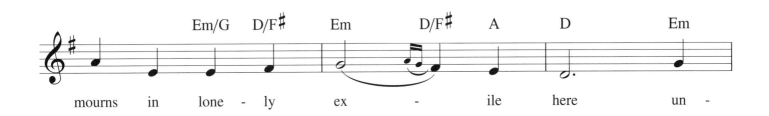

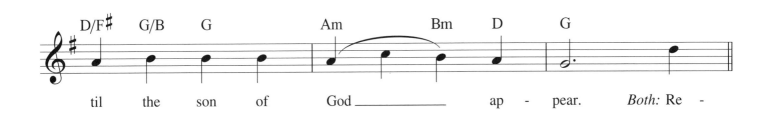

Refrain

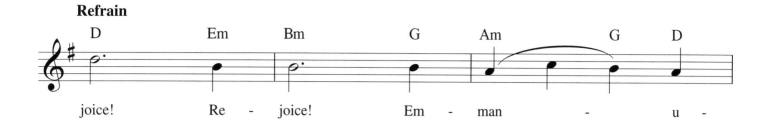

joice! Re - joice! Em - man - u -

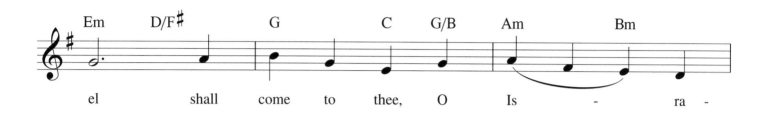

el shall come to thee, O Is - ra -

Verse 2

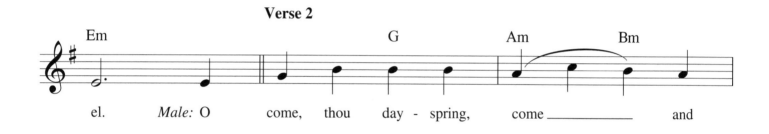

el. *Male:* O come, thou day - spring, come _____ and

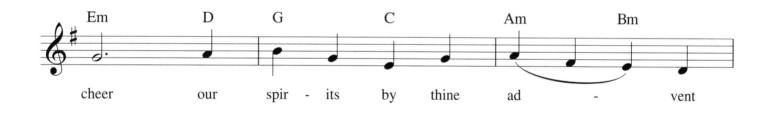

cheer our spir - its by thine ad - vent

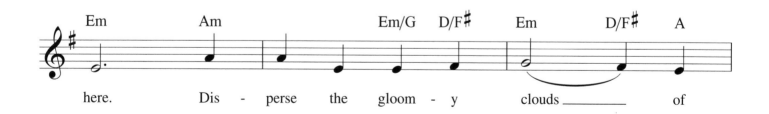

here. Dis - perse the gloom - y clouds _____ of

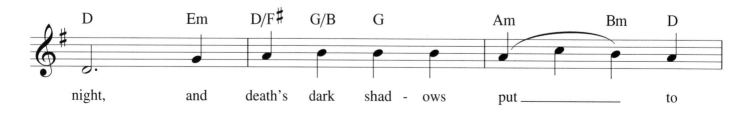

night, and death's dark shad - ows put _____ to

Refrain

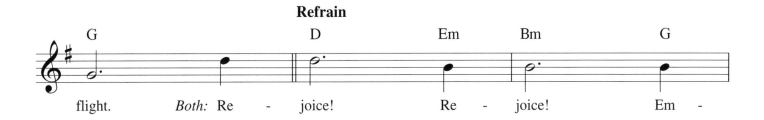

flight. *Both:* Re - joice! Re - joice! Em -

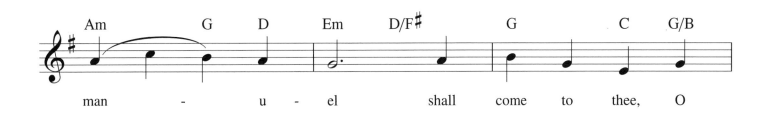

man - u - el shall come to thee, O

Verse 3

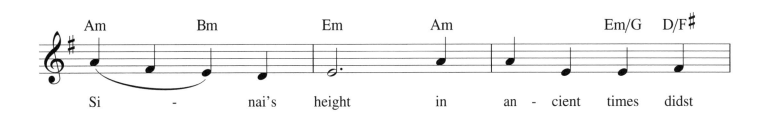

Is - ra - el. *Male:* O come, O come, thou

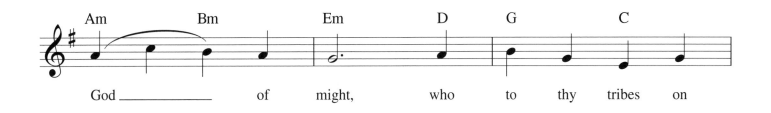

God _____ of might, who to thy tribes on

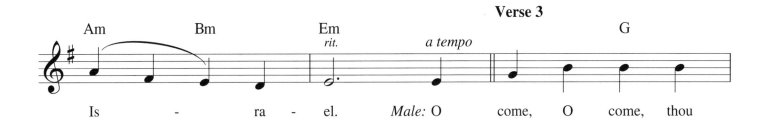

Si - nai's height in an - cient times didst

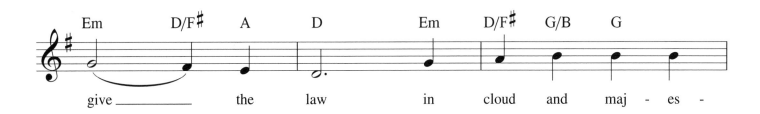

give _____ the law in cloud and maj - es -

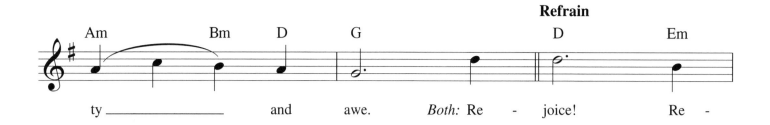

Refrain

ty _____ and awe. *Both:* Re - joice! Re -

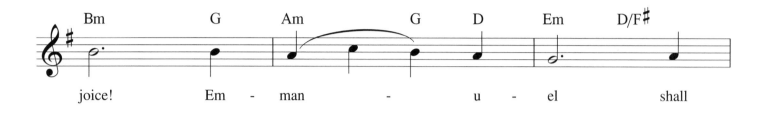

joice! Em - man - u - el shall

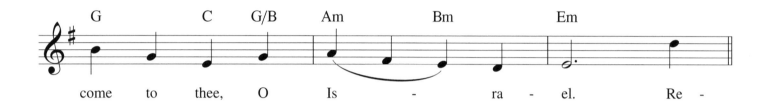

come to thee, O Is - ra - el. Re -

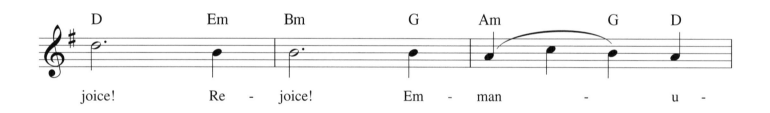

joice! Re - joice! Em - man - u -

el shall come to thee, O Is - ra -

el. _____

O Holy Night

French Words by Placide Cappeau
English Words by John S. Dwight
Music by Adolphe Adam

Intro
Gently, steadily   **Verse**

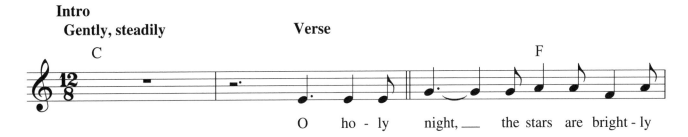

O ho - ly night, ___ the stars are bright - ly

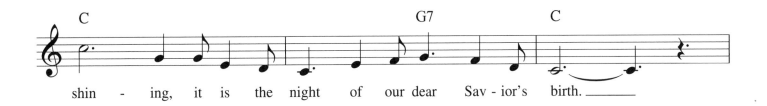

shin - ing, it is the night of our dear Sav - ior's birth. ___

Long lay the world ___ in sin and er - ror pin - ing, 'til he ap -

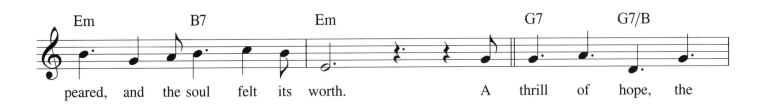

peared, and the soul felt its worth. A thrill of hope, the

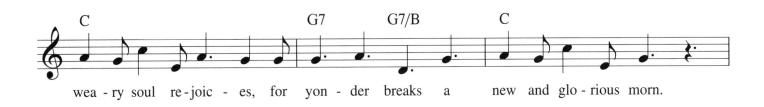

wea - ry soul re - joic - es, for yon - der breaks a new and glo - rious morn.

Fall ___ on your knees, ___ oh, hear ___ the an - gel

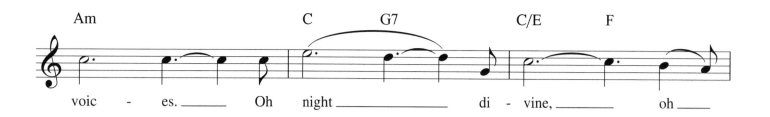

voic - es. _____ Oh night _____ di - vine, _____ oh _____

night _____ when Christ was born. _____ Oh night, _____ oh

ho - ly night, oh night di - vine.

Verse

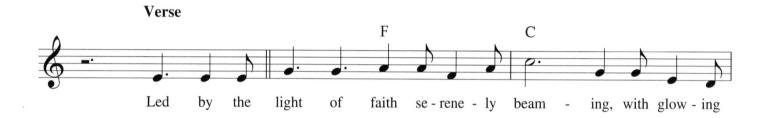

Led by the light of faith se - rene - ly beam - ing, with glow - ing

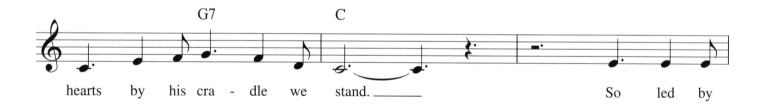

hearts by his cra - dle we stand. _____ So led by

light of a star sweet - ly gleam - ing, here came the wise men from Or - i - ent

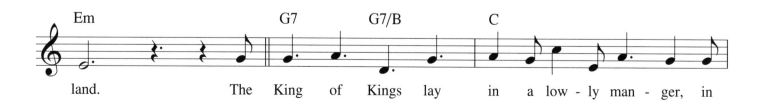

land. The King of Kings lay in a low - ly man - ger, in

all our tri - als born to be our friend. He _____ knows our

need, _____ to our weak - ness no stran - ger. _____ Be -

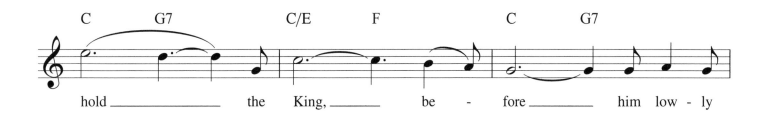

hold _____ the King, _____ be - fore _____ him low - ly

bend. _____ Be - hold _____ your King, _____ your

Verse

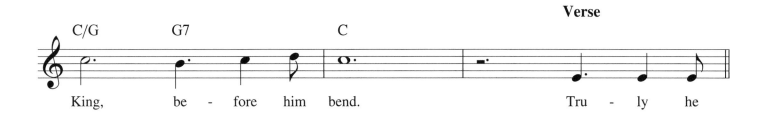

King, be - fore him bend. Tru - ly he

taught us to love one an - oth - er, his law is love, and his gos - pel is

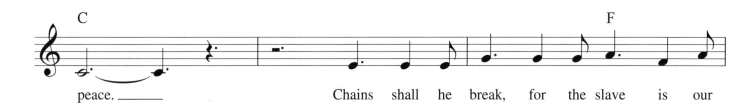

peace. _____ Chains shall he break, for the slave is our

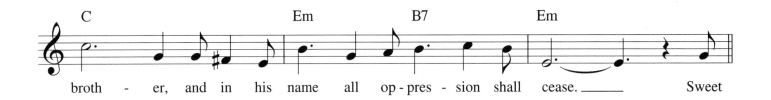

broth - er, and in his name all op-pres - sion shall cease. _____ Sweet

hymns of joy in grate - ful cho - rus raise we, let all with - in us

praise his ho - ly name. Christ _____ is the

Lord, _____ then ev - er, ev - er praise we. _____ His

pow'r _____ and glo - ry ____ ev - er more pro -

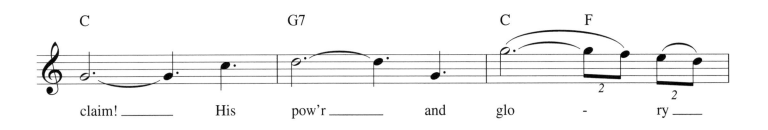

claim! _____ His pow'r _____ and glo - ry ____

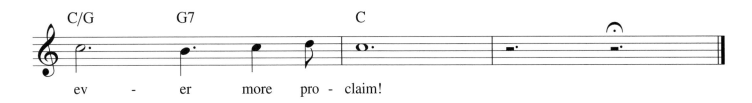

ev - er more pro - claim!

O Little Town Of Bethlehem

Words by Phillips Brooks
Music by Lewis H. Redner

Intro
Moderately

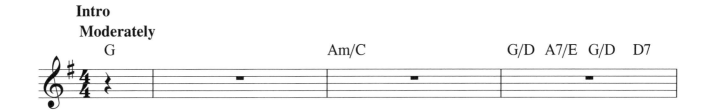

Verse 1

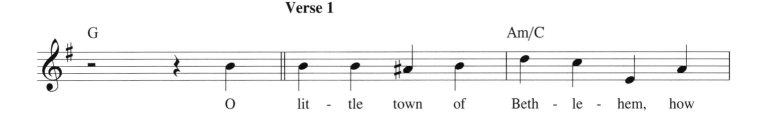

O lit - tle town of Beth - le - hem, how

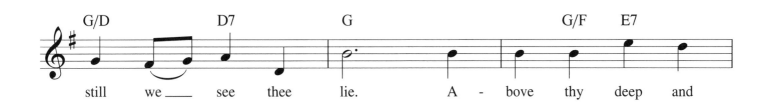

still we ___ see thee lie. A - bove thy deep and

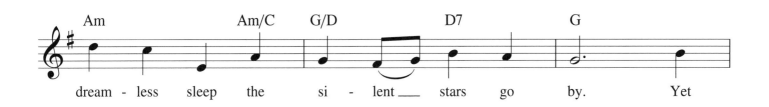

dream - less sleep the si - lent ___ stars go by. Yet

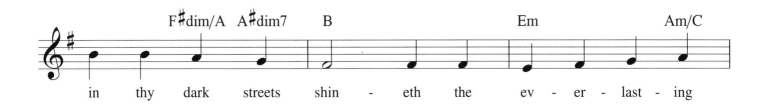

in thy dark streets shin - eth the ev - er - last - ing

light. The hopes and fears of all the years are

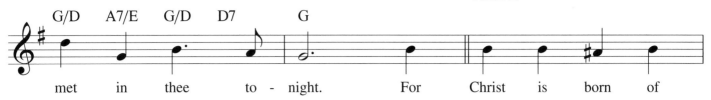

met in thee to - night. For Christ is born of

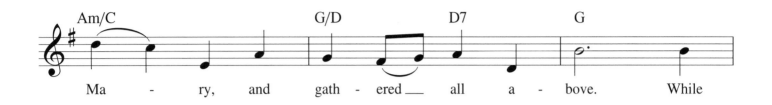

Ma - ry, and gath - ered ___ all a - bove. While

mor - tals sleep, the an - gels keep their watch of ___ won - d'ring

love. Oh morn - ing stars to - geth - er, pro -

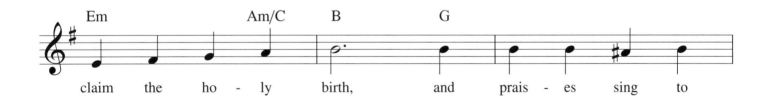

claim the ho - ly birth, and prais - es sing to

God our King, and peace to men on earth. O

Verse 3

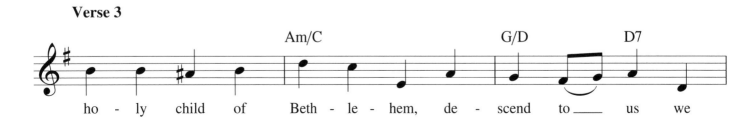

ho - ly child of Beth - le - hem, de - scend to ___ us we

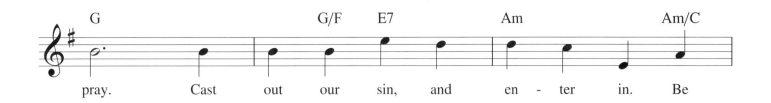

pray.   Cast   out   our   sin,   and   en - ter   in.   Be

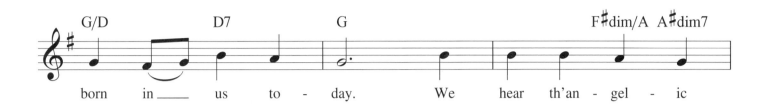

born   in ____ us   to - day.   We   hear   th'an - gel - ic

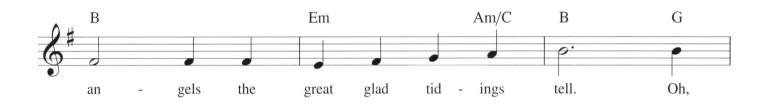

an - gels   the   great   glad   tid - ings   tell.   Oh,

come   to   us,   a - bide   with   us,   our   Lord   Em - man - u -

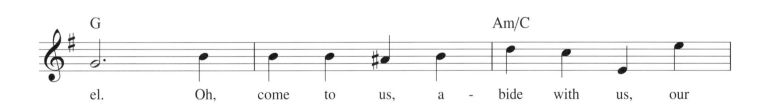

el.   Oh,   come   to   us,   a - bide   with   us,   our

Lord   Em - man - u - el.

The Twelve Days Of Christmas

Traditional English Carol

Intro
Moderately

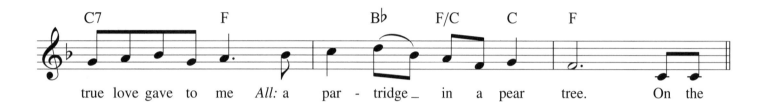

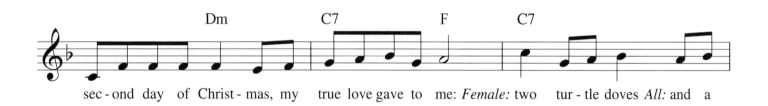

** The vocal parts can be divided up as the performer desires.
These indications match the recording.*

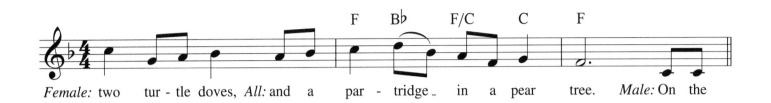

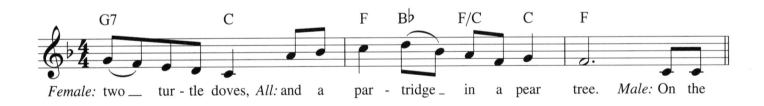

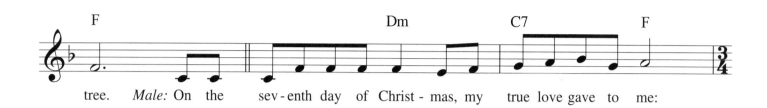

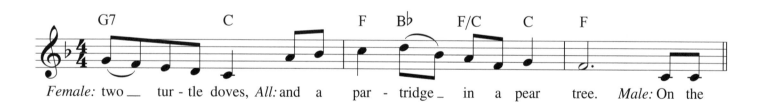

rings, *Female:* four ___ call - ing birds, *Male:* three French hens,

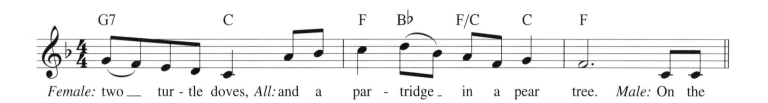

Female: two ___ tur - tle doves, *All:* and a par - tridge ___ in a pear tree. *Male:* On the

ninth day of Christ - mas, my true love gave to me: *Female:* nine la - dies danc - ing,

eight maids a - milk - ing, *Male:* sev - en swans a - swim - ming, *Female:* six geese a - lay - ing,

All: five gold - en rings, *Female:* four ___ call - ing birds,

Male: three French hens, *Female:* two ___ tur - tle doves, *All:* and a par - tridge ___ in a pear

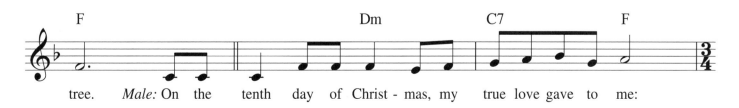

tree. *Male:* On the tenth day of Christ - mas, my true love gave to me:

ten   lords a - leap - ing,   *Female:* nine   la - dies danc - ing,   eight   maids a - milk - ing,

Male: sev - en swans a - swim - ming, *Female:* six   geese a - lay - ing, *All:* five   gold - en

rings,   *Female:* four ___ call - ing birds, *Male:* three   French   hens,

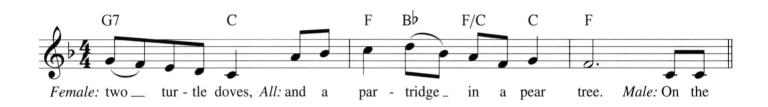

Female: two ___ tur - tle doves, *All:* and   a   par - tridge ___ in   a   pear   tree. *Male:* On the

'lev - enth day of Christ - mas, my   true love gave to   me: *Female:* 'lev - en pip - ers pip - ing,

Male: ten   lords a - leap - ing, *Female:* nine   la - dies danc - ing,   eight   maids a - milk - ing,

Male: sev - en swans a - swim - ming, *Female:* six   geese a - lay - ing, *All:* five   gold - en

rings, *Female:* four __ call - ing birds, *Male:* three French hens,

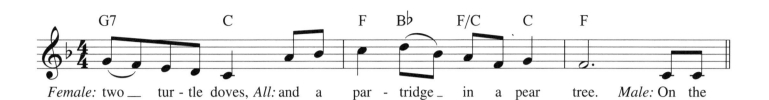

Female: two __ tur - tle doves, *All:* and a par - tridge __ in a pear tree. *Male:* On the

twelfth day of Christ - mas, my true love gave to me: *Female:* twelve drum - mers drum - ming,

'lev - en pip - ers pip - ing, *Male:* ten lords a - leap - ing, *Female:* nine la - dies danc - ing,

eight maids a - milk - ing, *Male:* sev - en swans a - swim - ming, *Female:* six geese a - lay - ing,

All: five gold - en rings, *Female:* four __ call - ing birds,

Male: three French hens, *Female:* two __ tur - tle doves, *Male:* and a par - tridge in a pear

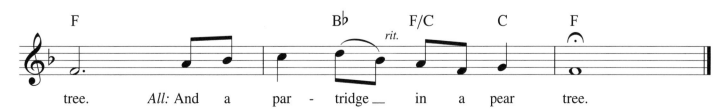

tree. *All:* And a par - tridge __ in a pear tree.

Pro Vocal® Series
SONGBOOK & SOUND-ALIKE CD
SING 8 GREAT SONGS
WITH A PROFESSIONAL BAND

Whether you're a karaoke singer or an auditioning professional, the Pro Vocal® series is for you! Unlike most karaoke packs, each book in the Pro Vocal Series contains the lyrics, melody, and chord symbols for eight hit songs. The CD contains demos for listening, and separate backing tracks so you can sing along. The CD is playable on any CD player, but it is also enhanced so PC and Mac computer users can adjust the recording to any pitch without changing the tempo! Perfect for home rehearsal, parties, auditions, corporate events, and gigs without a backup band.

MIXED EDITIONS
These editions feature songs for both male and female voices.

FOR MORE INFORMATION, SEE YOUR LOCAL MUSIC DEALER, OR WRITE TO:

HAL•LEONARD®
CORPORATION
7777 W. BLUEMOUND RD. P.O. BOX 13819 MILWAUKEE, WI 53213

Visit Hal Leonard online at www.halleonard.com

0509